Table of Contents

INTRODUCTION

Apple has always had a way to improve on customers' needs and desires in a gadget and as such, launched a new member of the iPad Pro lineup on March, 18th 2020. Presenting a faster A12Z Bionic processor, a new LiDAR scanner for improved augmented reality capabilities, an optional Magic Keyboard accessory that adds a trackpad to the iPad for the first time, improved audio, and dual rear cameras, the iPad Pro 2020 seems to be the most advanced iPad Pro to date, with several "pro" improvements for those who want an iPad that's able to replace a computer.

Just like the 2018 iPad Pro models, the iPad Pro 2020 design is unchanged. It is available in 11-inch and 12.9-inch sizes with an edge-to-edge display and an all-screen design that does not include a Home button. It features a TrueDepth camera system which enables the utilization of face recognition for biometric identification

(Face ID) and a 7-megapixel camera for selfies. The only real difference in the design of this new model from the older ones is the presence of a new rear camera system. There are two cameras; a 12-megapixel wide-angle camera and a 10-megapixel ultra-wide-angle camera that can zoom out about two times for a wider field of view.

This book is geared towards providing insight and in-depth knowledge about this new iPad Pro 2020 as well as serve as a user guide thus making the new iPad Pro 2020 your best choice and possible replacement for your PC.

DESIGN AND AVAILABILITY

The 2020 iPad Pro continues to look like the 2018 iPad Pro models as it didn't receive any major design refreshes. The iPad Pro is available in two sizes: 11 inches and 12.9 inches.

The 11-inch iPad Pro measures in at 9.74 inches in length, 7.02 inches wide and weighs in at 1.04 pounds, while the 12.9-inch iPad Pro measures in at 11.04 inches in length, 8.46 inches wide and weighs 1.41 pounds. Both iPad Pro 2020 models measure 5.9mm thick.

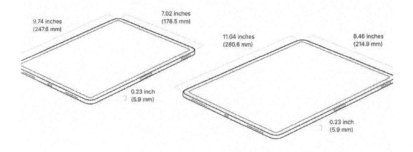

Apple offers the iPad Pro models in two colors; a Silver or Space Gray aluminum.

The 2020 iPad Pro models feature an edge-to-edge display with 6mm bezels at the top, sides, and bottom thus, it has no Home button. In place of the Touch ID home button, the iPad Pro uses a TrueDepth camera system with facial recognition capabilities for biometric authentication with the TrueDepth camera located in the top bezel of the iPad Pro. Still on the design, this iPad rather than having smooth, tapered edges, it has a more industrial-like band around the sides like the design of the iPhone 4 or the iPhone SE.

At the top of the iPad Pro, there are two speakers and a power button. On the right side of the device, there are volume buttons, a Nano-SIM tray on cellular iPads, and a magnetic connector. Just like older models, there is no headphone jack on the iPad Pro and as such headphones that work with USB-C or Bluetooth headphones are required.

The major change in the design of this iPad lies at its back where it features a square-shaped camera bump housing two cameras (a 12-megapixels wide-angle camera and a 10-megapixels ultra-wide-angle camera), a True Tone flash and the new LiDAR Scanner.

At the bottom of the iPad Pro, there's a USB-C port for charging and connecting accessories. This port allows the iPad Pro to be connected to digital cameras, 4K or 5K displays, and other USB-C devices. The USB-C port can be used to charge an iPhone or Apple Watch with the appropriate cable and supports USB 3.1 Gen 2 transfer speeds. The iPad Pro is available in Wi-Fi only or Cellular plus Wi-Fi. All the iPad Pro 2020 models feature a 6GB RAM capacity.

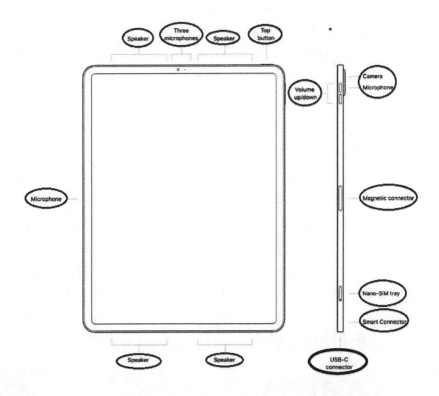

THE A12Z BIONIC SYSTEM ON CHIP

The 2020 iPad Pro presents an upgraded version of the A12X chip featured in the 2018 iPad Pro models. It features the A12Z Bionic chip which makes the iPad extremely fast even faster than some PCs. It has an 8-core CPU, an enhanced thermal architecture, tuned performance controllers, and especially an upgraded 8-core GPU. The A12Z also incorporates a Neural Engine that's able to perform five trillion operations per second. The Neural Engine powers the entire machine learning features in the iPad Pro, like allows for faster Face ID facial recognition, faster plane detection for augmented reality apps and objects, photo search, speed improvements for other tasks that use real-time machine learning, and it powers the LiDAR sensor in the iPad Pro. *Now you know why this iPad is extremely fast!*

CAMERAS

The iPad Pro 2020 features a front-facing 7-megapixel camera built into the top bezel of the iPad Pro, for selfies and FaceTime videos. It also supports

Portrait Mode, Portrait Lighting, and Animoji and Memoji. It also features two rear cameras; a 12-megapixel wide-angle camera with an aperture of f/1.8 and a 10-megapixel ultra-wide-angle camera with an aperture of f/2.4 and a 125-degree field of view. The ultra-wide-angle camera allows for different perspectives and multi-camera use as it can zoom out two times for a much wider field of view thus doubling the video and photo possibilities. The iPad Pro can record 4K video up to 60fps with either camera, and it also supports time-lapse video, slo-mo video, and cinematic video stabilization when recording at 720 or 1080p. Other supported features include; Smart HDR, Quad-LED True Tone Flash, wide color, burst mode, noise reduction, Live Photos, auto image stabilization, and 63-megapixel panoramas.

DISPLAY

Still using the same "Liquid Retina" edge-to-edge display technology that was available in the 2018 iPad Pro models, the iPad Pro 2020 features a wide color gamut (ensures vivid colors that are natural and accurate), True Tone for adjusting to ambient light, ProMotion 120Hz refresh capabilities (which makes motion content on the screen smoother, and more responsive for gaming, watching/streaming movies, and reading) and an anti-reflective coating. The 11-inch iPad Pro has a resolution of 2388 x 1668, while the 12.9-inch model has a resolution of 2732 x 2048 with both having a pixel density of 264PPI like older models.

FACE ID

The iPad Pro 2020 uses the Face to unlock iPad, allow access to third-party passcode-protected apps, confirm purchases, and authenticate Apple Pay payments. This is possible, as the Face ID uses sensors and cameras built into the top bezel of the iPad Pro (TrueDepth camera system) to create a scan of your face that's used for authentication purposes.

HOW DOES IT WORK?

A dot projector projects over 30,000 invisible infrared dots onto the user's face and immediately, the dot map is read by an infrared camera and the structure of the user's face is relayed to the A12Z Bionic processor where it is transformed into a mathematical model and the Face ID is encrypted and stored in the Secure Enclave of the A12Z chip not on cloud or sent to Apple or even accessible by apps. This technology is more secure than the Touch ID, and it is unable to be fooled by a mask, photo, or other facial imitation. The Face ID is very efficient as it is designed to work in the dark when wearing sunglasses, and even with the face partially obscured by scarves, makeup, and other accessories. It can work in either portrait or landscape orientation, unlike iPhones that Face ID can only work in portrait orientation.

LiDAR SCANNER

Occupying the square-shaped camera bump with the two-camera setup is the new LiDAR Scanner (Light Detection and Ranging) that uses reflected light to measure the distance of objects up to five meters away in nano-second speeds.

This is very interesting as it has enabled capabilities that were never thought possible on smartphones. Augmented reality experiences on the iPad Pro 2020 just became more top-notch. *How so?*

Apple explains that new depth frameworks present in the iPadOS combine depth points from the LiDAR scanner with data from cameras and motion sensors handled by the A12Z Bionic chip to create a whole new AR experience on the iPad Pro as existing ARKit apps will get improved motion capture and instant AR placement. This LiDAR Scanner also improved the Measure app as it can now automatically calculate a person's height and object measurements are faster and more accurate than never before.

BATTERY

Both iPad Pro 2020 models feature a Non-removable rechargeable Li-Po battery. The 11-inch iPad Pro has a 28.65-watt-hour battery while the 12.9-inch iPad Pro has a 36.71-watt-hour battery both of which offer up to 10 hours of battery life while watching a video or surfing the internet. The battery is charged with a USB-C Lightning cable using an 18W power adapter.

MICROPHONE AND SPEAKERS

The iPad Pro 2020 features five studio-quality microphones and four speakers (two at the top and two at the bottom). This enables capturing super clean audio quality and the quietest details from the surroundings and also adjusts the sound to any orientation for the better hearing experience.

Wi-Fi AND BLUETOOTH

The iPad Pro 2020 models support Wi-Fi 6, also known as 802.11ax. This allows for improved network capacity, faster speeds, lower latency, better power efficiency, and upgraded connectivity when there are multiple Wi-Fi devices in the same area. It also supports Bluetooth 5.0 which offers faster speed, larger broadcast message capacity, and longer range.

OTHER FEATURES

The iPad Pro 2020 supports the Dual-Sim functionality as it allows the use of a physical Nano-SIM and an eSIM. As regards storage, the iPad Pro can starts out with 128GB and be upgraded up to 1TB. Another important feature is the Smart Connector on the back of the iPad Pro designed to allow it to communicate with and power accessories like the Smart Keyboard Folio.

ACCESSORIES

MAGIC KEYBOARD/TRACKPAD

Apple brings the best typing experience ever on iPad with the new version of the Smart Keyboard; the Magic Keyboard. The design of the Magic Keyboard allows the iPad to "float in the air" when used in keyboard mode. It has a folio-style case that folds and protects the iPad when not in use.

This Magic keyboard features a trackpad, backlit keys, and a scissor-switch mechanism with 1mm of key travel. It attaches magnetically to the iPad Pro and features cantilevered hinges that allow for smooth viewing angle adjustments up to about 130 degrees. The Magic keyboard has a USB-C port for pass-through inductive USB-C charging capabilities thus leaving the iPad Pro's USB-C port free for accessories like external drives.

The trackpad present is supported by iPadOS 13.4. Trackpad support is designed as a touch-first experience. The cursor appears as a circle but shifts to highlight user interface elements like apps on the Home screen, text fields, and other items letting the user know what can be clicked on. Users can switch between apps, activate the Control Center, Dock, and apps in Slide Over via gestures designed on the trackpad. The trackpad support is so designed that it supports both first and third-party apps. For example, scrolling through web pages in Safari, scrolling, and selecting photo libraries in Photos, viewing emails in Mail, writing, and editing text in Notes.

APPLE PENCIL

The iPad Pro 2020 supports the second-generation Apple Pencil that was introduced in 2018. The Apple Pencil pairs and charges inductively when attached magnetically to the iPad Pro. Gesture support is also included with the second-generation Apple Pencil as with a double-tap, the user can change quickly switch tools (i.e. from a brush to an eraser) without having to pick up the pencil to select a new tool. Pressure support allows thinner and thicker lines to be drawn by increasing the amount of pressure on the iPad's screen. Surely, this pencil is easy and ready to use for note-taking, drawing, and marking up documents on your iPad Pro 2020.

HOW TO SET UP YOUR IPAD PRO 2020

Now that you have gotten this your new iPad Pro, setting up might just be an issue especially if new to the iOS family. In this regard, you need to know your options when setting up. These options include;

- Setting up new - This is for people who've never used an iPad or any iOS device or want their device brand new.

- Restoring from a previous or iPad - This is for people who've had a previous iOS device and want to transfer everything they had on the older device unto the new device. This is possible with iCloud backups or with iTunes.

- Importing data from a non-iOS device (Android) - This is for people switching from a different non-iOS platform to an iPad.

- Having fully understood your options, please ensure that before the setting up process begins proper, the following should be carried out for a seamless process;
- There must be an available Cellular network.
- In the absence of a Cellular network, a Wi-Fi network should be available.
- Ensure the iPad is charged. If the battery is drained, please charge.

SETTING UP AS A NEW IPAD

- Turn on your new iPad - Press and hold the power button until the Apple logo appears.
- Immediately, "Hello" in different languages would display on the screen. Swipe your finger across the screen of your iPad to get started properly.
- Choose your preferred language.
- Choose your country or region.
- Click "Set Up manually".
- Select a Cellular Network or a Wi-Fi network depending on which is available at the moment of set up.
- Tap "Continue" after reading Apple's Data & Privacy information.
- Choose "Continue" and follow the instructions to set up Face ID or click "Set Up Face ID Later in settings".

- Create a Passcode - Enter a six-digit passcode or to use a custom passcode, tap "Passcode Options." This allows you to use some features like Face ID, Apple pay, make some App purchases.
- Re-type the passcode you created and press "Next".
- A list of options on how to transfer apps and data to the iPad Pro would pop up on the screen. Click on Don't Transfer Apps & Data.
- Input Apple ID and Password. If you don't have an existing ID or want to create a new one, just Tap *Don't have an Apple ID?* and follow the instructions. Click Next.
- Apple's Terms and Conditions, click "Agree".
- Express Settings – You can choose to use the default settings by clicking "Continue" or edit the settings individually by clicking "Customize Settings" depending on

how you want to handle your privacy.

- Click "Continue" to get the latest update to install automatically by or click "Install Update Manually" to install manually.
- Apple Pay – Click "Continue" to Set up Apple Pay or click Set Up Later in Wallet.
- Click "Continue" to Set up Siri and "Hey, Siri" or Click Set it Up Later in Settings.
- Click "Continue" to Set up Screen Time or Click "Set it Up in Settings".
- App Analytics - Click Share with App Developers or Don't Share (clicking "Don't share" saves battery life and maintains your privacy).
- Choose the color tone you want on your iPad and click "Continue".
- Select Display mode (Dark or Light) mode. Click "Continue".

- "Go Home" display - On your screen Click Continue.
- Just tap on "Continue" to go to the next display until you see "Welcome to iPad". Swipe up to get started.

RESTORING FROM A PREVIOUS IPAD

Another way of setting up your new device is by using QuickStart. This is possible if your old iPad and new iPad are operating on iPadOS 11, 12.4, 13, or later (Note the iPad Pro 2020 is shipped with iPadOS 13.4 so it is compatible with this process). This procedure allows you to transfer information swiftly from your old device to the new device wirelessly in a few minutes. For this to work effectively, either iPads needs to have a charge or plugged into power as this process occupies both ipads. This means that any form of interruption (battery drain) could affect the data transfer. You should have a backup for your data (iCloud or iTunes) especially if you are running on older iPadOS (11, 12.4) on your old device before starting this quick start process to enable full data transfer your new iPad. However, if your old device is running on iPadOS 13 and later, the need for a backup won't be necessary (as all your data would be transferred from your old to a new device) except you just want to.

HOW TO USE QUICK START FOR DATA TRANSFER

- Turn on your new iPad - Press and hold the power button until the Apple logo appears.
- Immediately, "Hello" in different languages would display on the screen. Swipe your finger across the screen to start proper.
- Choose your preferred language.
- Put your new iPad close near your old iPad that's running iPadOS 11 or later.
- Immediately, the QuickStart screen would display on your old iPad and

offer the option of using your Apple ID (the ID logged in your old device) to set up your new iPad.

- Input your Apple ID you want to use.
- Click "Continue". If you fail to see the option to continue on your old iPad screen, ensure that the Bluetooth is turned on.
- Immediately an animated image would appear on your new iPad.
- Place and hold your old iPad over the new iPad, then center the viewfinder of your old iPad on the animated image.
- A pop-up message that says Finish would appear on your new iPad.
- Input your old device's passcode on your new device.
- After that, follow the instructions to set up Face ID or click Set Up Face ID Later in settings.
- Select from two options either download data from iCloud or

transfer data from the old iPad. I advise that you, Click on "Transfer data from iPad" most especially if your old device is running on iPadOS 13 and later because it is quicker.

- Apple's Terms and Conditions, click "Agree".
- Express Settings – You can choose to use the default settings by clicking "Continue" or edit the settings individually by clicking "Customize Settings" depending on how you want to handle your privacy.
- Click "Continue" to get the latest update to install automatically by or click "Install Update Manually" to install manually.
- Apple Pay – Click "Continue" to Set up Apple Pay or click Set Up Later in Wallet.

- Click "Continue" to Set up Siri and "Hey, Siri" or Click Set it Up Later in Settings.
- Click "Continue" to Set up Screen Time or Click "Set it Up in Settings".
- App Analytics - Click Share with App Developers or Don't Share (clicking "Don't share" saves battery life and maintains your privacy).
- Select Display mode (Dark or Light) mode. Click "Continue".
- A transfer progress bar pops-up occupies the screen of both iPads.
- After the completion of the entire transfer process a message saying "Transfer complete" pops up on the old iPad.
- Immediately, the new device would reboot with Apps downloading in the background.

In minutes, all your data (Photos, Videos, Contacts, and App data) are now on your new iPad Pro 2020.

IMPORTING DATA FROM A NON-iOS DEVICE (ANDROID)

There are non-iOS smartphone users all over the world who are on an Android-based operating system and want to share in the Apple experience. This means they would want to transfer all their data and files from their older smartphone to this new iPadOS platform. This is good news, as Apple has an app in Google Playstore that makes this possible and very easy. That's great! The app is called *Move to iOS* and should already be downloaded and installed on the Android device you wish to transfer from.

HOW DOES THIS TRANSFER WORK?

This is works through a direct connection (Wi-Fi) between the iOS device and the Android device. This connection is only possible also when the iPad is running on iOS 9 and higher and the *Move to iOS* app is already installed on the android device. This process does not transfer music, apps, or any of your saved passwords. It only transfers photos, accounts, contacts, and calendars.

PROCEDURE FOR THE TRANSFER

- Turn on your new iPad - Press and hold the power button until the Apple logo appears.
- Immediately, "Hello" in different languages would display on the screen. Swipe your finger across the screen of your iPad to get started properly.
- Choose your preferred language.
- Choose your country or region.
- Click "Set Up manually".

- Choose a Cellular Network or a Wi-Fi network Cellular Network depending on which is available at the moment of set up.
- Tap "Continue" after reading Apple's Data & Privacy information.
- Choose "Continue" and follow the instructions to set up Face ID or click "Set Up Face ID Later in settings".
- Create a Passcode - Enter a six-digit passcode or to use a custom passcode, tap "Passcode Options." This allows you to use some features like Face ID, Apple pay, make some App purchases.
- Re-type the passcode you created and press Next.
- Transfer of App & Data - Set up options on how to transfer apps and data to the iPad would be displayed on the screen.

- Click on "Move Data from Android".
- Launch the *Move to iOS* app on the Android device.
- Click "Continue" on both the Android device and the iPad.
- Click Agree on the Android device and then click Next.
- Input a 12-digit code displayed on the iPad into the Android device.
- Having entered the code correctly, the Android device would then automatically connect with the iPad via Wi-Fi.
- A transfer list of what you would want to transfer from the Android device would appear. Select on all or any and Tap "Continue".
- After transfer completion, Click on Continue Setting Up iPad.
- Input Apple ID and Password. If you don't have an existing ID or want to create a new one, just Tap *Don't have an Apple ID?* and

follow the instructions. Click "Next".

- Apple's Terms and Conditions, Click Agree.
- Express Settings – You can choose to use the default settings by clicking "Continue" or edit the settings individually by clicking "Customize Settings" depending on how you want to handle your privacy.
- Click "Continue" to get the latest update to install automatically by or click "Install Update Manually" to install manually.
- Apple Pay – Tap "Continue" to Set up Apple Pay or click "Set Up Later in Wallet".
- Click "Continue" to Set up Siri and "Hey, Siri" or Tap Set it Up Later in Settings.
- Click "Continue" to Set up Screen Time or Click "Set it Up in Settings".

- App Analytics - Click Share with App Developers or Don't Share (clicking "Don't share" saves battery life and maintains your privacy).
- Select the desired Tone display.
- Select Display mode (Dark or Light) mode. Click "Continue".
- "Go Home" display - On your screen Click Continue.
- Just tap on "Continue" to go to the next display until you see "Welcome to iPad". Swipe up to get started.
- You would see a pop-up asking you to log into the accounts that were transferred from the Android device to your iPad.
- After doing this, you are ready to enjoy your new iPad!

HOW TO SET UP FACE ID

Apple's facial identity scanner has proven to be the best and most secure means of authentication. It unlocks the iPad pro, secure apps, and authenticate Apple pay, some App purchases.

If you skipped setting up Face ID when setting up your iPad, there practically no need to worry. Heed these basic steps below for a successful set up:

- Open the Settings app on your iPad Pro.
- Click on Face ID & Passcode.
- Enter your Passcode.
- Click on Set Up Face ID.
- Click on Get Started.
- Position your face inside the circle.
- Slowly move your head in a circle.
- Click on Continue.
- Slowly move your head in a second circle.
- Click on Done to finish.

HOW TO SET UP AND ADD A SECOND PERSON TO FACE ID

Ordinarily, Apple made provision for setting up an Alternative Appearance for devices that uses the Face ID. It targeted people that may temporarily have altered their appearance probably from surgery or some other reason. However, you can use it to set up a second person to unlock your iPad Pro using the Face ID.

- Launch the Settings app on your iPad Pro.
- Click on Face ID & Passcode.
- Enter your Passcode.
- Click on Set up an Alternate Appearance.
- Click on Get Started.
- Then place your face inside the circle.

- Move your head slowly in the circle.
- Click on Continue.
- Slowly move your head in a second circle.
- Click on Done to finish.

HOW TO TRANSFER FILES FROM YOUR MAC TO YOUR IPAD PRO

Follow these easy steps below to transfer your files from your Mac to your iPad seamlessly;

- Plug your iPad into your Mac using the supplied cable.
- Launch a Finder window by clicking the Finder icon in the Dock.
- Click your iPad device's name in the sidebar.
- Click Trust in the Finder window.

- Click Trust on your iPad when prompted, and then enter your passcode to confirm.
- Click on the Files tab to see a list of apps that can share files. If you don't see a Files section, your iPad doesn't have any apps that can share files.
- Press Command-N on your Mac to open another Finder window and select the files on your Mac that you want to copy to your iPad. Select files that work with an app on your iPad.
- Drag the file(s) to the compatible app on your iPad device. Finder will then automatically copy them across to your iPad. The duration of the transfer would depend on the size of the file(s) so you may have to wait a while for the transfer to complete.

HOW TO TRANSFER FILES FROM YOUR IPAD PRO TO YOUR MAC

Follow these easy steps below to transfer your files from your iPad to your Mac seamlessly;

- Plug your iPad into your Mac using the supplied cable.
- Launch a Finder window by clicking the Finder icon in the Dock.
- Click your iPad device's name in the sidebar.
- Click Trust in the Finder window.
- Click Trust on your iPad when prompted, and then enter your passcode to confirm.
- Click on the Files tab to see a list of apps that can share files. If you don't see a Files section, your iPad doesn't have any apps that can share files.

- Click on the triangle next to an app to see the files that you can share.
- Press Command-N on your Mac to open another Finder window and navigate to the location on your Mac where you'd like to copy the files on your iPad.
- Select the files on your iPad that you want to copy.
- Drag the file(s) to the open location on your Mac in the other Finder window.
- Finder will then automatically copy the files across to your Mac. The duration of the transfer would depend on the size of the file(s) so you may have to wait a while for the transfer to complete.

HOW TO SET UP YOUR EMAIL ON YOUR IPAD PRO

Having gotten your new iPad and it's all set up; the next thing for you might be setting up your email so you can start sending emails and also start making purchases from the App Store with an iTunes ID. The iPad almost automates the email setup especially if you have an already existing email account. If you have a Gmail, Yahoo!, iCloud, Exchange, Hotmail, AOL account, or another type of mail, the Mail app gives you access to these accounts as well as signing in through the safari browser. After the setup, you can use Mail to write, retrieve, and forward messages. Below are steps that would run this setup in a few minutes;

- Launch the Settings app on the Home screen.

- In the Settings dialog, click Mail, Contacts, Calendars.
- Click Add Account.
- Click Gmail, Yahoo! Mail, Hotmail, iCloud, or AOL and then proceed to enter your account information in the format that appears.
- After entry, your iPad verifies your account information.
- Tap on Save. Your account is saved, and you can now open it using the Mail app.

TROUBLESHOOTING BATTERY PROBLEMS

Most times it can be very disappointing when you get a new device and suddenly the battery starts giving you issues already......it can be frustrating!!! However, some troubleshooting tips might just help resolve that issue.
When you get your new device, a lot of stuff and activities occur in the background especially when you just finished setting up a new device or from a backup. This is because you are probably still connected to a cellular network or Wi-Fi and you have iOS installing, apps downloading as well as emails, photos, and files. This translates to a lot of power consumption. So the first tip is;

Be patient- Give things a day or two to normalize then observe if it's normal. If the battery issue persists, try the next tip.

Standby- Most times you might be so engrossed with the new features of this new device that you might want to explore forgetting that you have been operating the device for so long. It's only natural that the battery drains as battery loss is dependent highly on usage. After usage, leave your iPad on standby. Wait for say 20-45minutes and observe your battery life. If there isn't a considerable difference from when you left on standby till when you picked it up, it means your battery is normal and would adjust to normal usage. If your battery continues to drain fast without you using it, try the next tip.

Rebooting/Restart- Rebooting or restarting the iPad might just do the trick. All you have to do is;

- Press and hold the top power button and either volume button (Up or Down) on your iPad.
- Continue holding them until the screen turns off.
- Continue holding them until you see the Apple logo appears.
- Release the buttons.

Still didn't work?

Try lowering power on iPad-Even though there isn't Low Power Mode for iPad as there is for iPhones, there's a lot you can do to reduce fast battery drain.

- Decrease screen brightness.
- Set Auto-Lock to 1 minute or even less.
- Use headphones instead of the speaker when listening to music.
- Turn off Lock screen notifications.
- Turn off push for mail and turn on fetch instead.
- Turn off Background Refresh for apps.

If the battery drain persists, the last option is the **nuclear option** that is restoring the iPad as new which means resetting the iPad.

- Navigate your way to the Settings app
- Launch the Settings app
- Tap on General
- Scroll down until you see "Reset"
- Tap Reset

- Then tap "Erase All Contents and Settings".
- Follow the prompt with the instructions and wait for your iPad to turn off.

www.ingramcontent.com/pod-product-compliance
Lightning Source LLC
LaVergne TN
LVHW041221050326
832903LV00021B/725